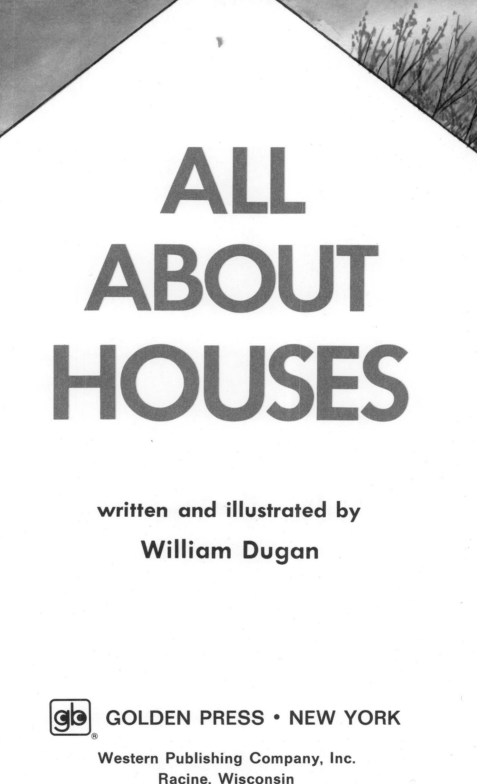

ALL ABOUT HOUSES

written and illustrated by

William Dugan

gb **GOLDEN PRESS • NEW YORK**

Western Publishing Company, Inc.
Racine, Wisconsin

Library of Congress Catalog Number: 74-25137

How Your House Grew

YOUR COMFORTABLE HOUSE

Your clock radio switches on. Music fills the room. Rolling over, you realize that a new day has begun. You hop out of bed, walk down the hall, switch on the bathroom light, brush your teeth, and then take a shower. After dressing, you are ready for breakfast. You pop two pieces of bread into the toaster and soon you are enjoying toast and marmalade with your milk. An ordinary day has begun in an ordinary way . . . or has it?

SOME NOT-SO-COMFORTABLE HOUSES

Such a day would seem anything but ordinary to vast numbers of people who are living today, for strange though it may seem, most of them have no clocks, no radios, and no electricity. More than half the people on earth have never had any source of light except fire, and to them, switching on a light as you did in your bathroom would seem a miracle.

People who must carry containers of water to their houses for cooking and washing would think it another miracle to get water by turning on a faucet and having water pour forth. They would certainly find it amazing to brown pieces of bread without any visible fire.

But to you who have always known radios, television sets, lamps, washing machines, driers, toasters, coffee makers, and other appliances, none of this seems at all unusual.

This book will try to show how extraordinary your house is in comparison with dwellings of the past, and even with many of those in the world today.

MAN'S FIRST SHELTERS

No one is quite sure how long humans have lived on earth, but recent discoveries in Africa show that it may be close to four million years. Some scientists believe four and a half million years may be more nearly correct.

From the very beginning, man has had three great needs: food, water, and shelter. In the begin-

ning of his history, he had to protect himself not only from the weather and from wild beasts, but also from other men. Often he found his shelter in

or under trees, or under bushes or rocks. Later, caves became his dwelling place. In addition to these natural homes, early man also learned to *build* shelters

by piling up stones or leaning branches of trees or bushes against one another. Sometimes he dug holes deep in the ground and found shelter there.

This cool desert house can be carried from place to place.

MAN THE BUILDER

As time went on, man learned to build shelters that were a bit more complicated, but these varied greatly from place to place. If man lived in a very hot area, he built a cool shelter. If he lived in a cold area, he built a tight warm house to keep out chilling winds. If he was a hunter who followed herds of wild animals, he'd need a house that he could pick up and carry along with him. In other words, the kind of shelter people preferred depended on the climate and the kind of life they lived.

But one other thing played a part in helping men decide what kinds of houses to build—this was the materials they could find nearby. In places where there were great forests, for example in what are now Canada and the northern parts of Europe and the United States, he made his dwellings of wood. In rockier places he used stone.

To this day, men build with whatever is nearby. About ten years ago, some young people started a community called Drop City, in Colorado. Being artists, writers, musicians, and filmmakers, who were beginners in their professions, they had little money, and so they had to use whatever materials were near at hand and, if possible, free. They tore down abandoned houses for the lumber, and found uses for tin cans, bottle caps, and factory-rejected plywood.

A house in Drop City

HOUSES MADE OF WOOD

One of the earliest shelters built by man was a cone-shaped hut. It consisted of branches that were first stuck into the earth to form a circle and then tied together at the top to make a pointed roof. Then the Stone Age house builder filled the spaces between the branches with reeds, bark, woven branches, mud, or hides. The tepee of some North American Indians was a dwelling of this type.

Another wooden structure built by primitive people looked like the conical hut, but it had a center post to give it strength. Early man was as inventive as we are, and he never gave up trying to improve on what he had, and so he also built huts with upright walls, in addition to the center post.

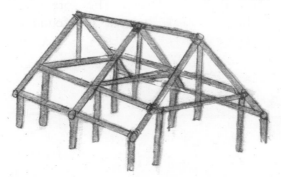

Huts that were still more complicated had upright walls and side posts, too.

HOUSES MADE OF STONE

Men also used stone to build their circular huts. In these the walls were made of piled-up rocks, held together by mortar, which at that time was probably mud or clay. The whole structure was roofed over with branches.

Another dwelling place, called the beehive hut, was so well built that some examples are still standing. The piled-up stones that formed its walls curved inward to make the roof.

Although these "houses" may not seem to us either comfortable or beautiful, we must remember that early men, women, and children spent little time indoors. During a large part of the day, the men hunted, while the women searched for seeds and roots to eat. The hut was used only for sleeping and as a shelter from the weather and enemies.

A broch or stone tower

A Tower House

Another dwelling of early man was the *broch,* a large tower that may have been used as a place of safety when enemies were about. Its very thick walls were made of stones, and its center was an open space where animals were perhaps kept. Of course, the broch also included rooms for human beings.

The Tepee

In very early times, several types of houses or shelters were built in the Americas. The *tepee* of the North American Plains Indians was one, the *adobe* of the Pueblo Indians another.

American Indians built the tepee mainly as a shelter that could be carried from place to place and could be easily put up and taken down. This made it possible for buffalo-hunting Indians of the central part of the United States to follow the herds for great distances, pitching the tepee wherever it was convenient.

The tepee was built on four supporting poles. Then, depending on its size, a number of other poles were placed around them. When these were all in place, the Indians covered the structure with hides, which were often decorated with paintings.

The tepee had one great advantage over the white man's tent: a fire could be built inside it because a hole was left at the top through which smoke could escape. This arrangement also permitted a kind of "air conditioning" in warm weather, for as the hot air rose and left the tepee through the hole, cooler air entered through the door opening.

Women built the tepee and kept it in repair.

An adobe house

ADOBE HOUSES

Some houses of the Indians of the southwestern United States were built of stones, which were then cemented together with *adobe,* a local clay. Other houses were made completely of adobe.

Before the coming of the Spaniards in the sixteenth century, the Pueblo Indians had not yet discovered that bricks could be made by pouring wet mud into a mold, and so they shaped them by hand. Such "bricks" were called *turtlebacks* because that's what they looked like. After the Indian builder placed the turtlebacks one upon the other, he cemented them together with adobe.

AN INDIAN APARTMENT HOUSE

An adobe dwelling was sometimes several stories high, but it had no doors or windows on the first floor. There was a good reason for this: when other tribes attacked an adobe village, they had no way of entering the doorless, windowless houses. A dwelling could be entered only by means of a ladder which could be pulled up in case of attack.

The Pueblo Indians were not a single tribe, but rather many tribes of peaceful farmers who, over the centuries, had come to follow the same way of life. About a thousand years ago, some savage and warlike tribes began to wander into Pueblo territory. These invaders were the ancestors of the Navajos and the Apaches.

It was probably partly to protect themselves from the newcomers that the Pueblo Indians built their cliff dwellings on *mesas* — flat-topped hills with steep, rocky sides. The wearing away of the steep hillsides formed deep hollows in the side of the hills. It was in these hollows that the Pueblo Indians built their towns. The people who lived in the houses used ladders to go up and down the cliff. The towns were easy to defend because, to attack them from below, an enemy had to climb the face of the cliff. But how could they do this when the ladders had all been pulled up?

HOUSES MADE OF SNOW

The way of life of the Eskimos of North America and Greenland was quite different from that of the Indians. The Eskimos had permanent homes, which were usually holes dug in the ground, covered with the rib bones of whales; between these, sod was placed to keep the house warm. But the Eskimos also needed dwellings to protect them from the bitter cold when they were on hunting trips or traveling for some other reason. The *igloo* supplied this need.

The igloo was made of blocks of snow that had been placed in a circle on the ground. As the blocks were laid one upon another, they were curved inward to form a dome.

Some clear blocks of ice were placed at the top of the igloo to allow light to filter through from the outside, but most of the time light came from stone or pottery lamps that burned seal or whale oil. Such lamps were also used for cooking. Of course, the igloo had no running water, but this was obtained by melting snow.

Most modern Eskimos have given up this form of shelter, but the igloo was still being used by some Eskimos in the very recent past.

People entered the igloo through a low tunnel.

11

MAN THE FARMER

Thus far, aside from such houses as the cliff dwellings of the Pueblo Indians, the houses we have seen were those of very early people who did not live in one place, but spent most of their time traveling about to find food. But as time went on, people learned to tame wild animals to supply meat and to grow on farms the grain they needed. After these great discoveries, families were no longer forced to wander from place to place in search of food, and they began to build permanent homes. These were usually placed together in villages as a protection against enemies.

THE FIRST TOWNS AND CITIES

Bricks of plain mud didn't last long, but someone discovered that if the clay bricks were dried they had a very long life. At first, bricks were dried in the sun; later they were baked in a kiln, a kind of oven.

In time large towns and cities grew, and they came to be ruled by governors and kings. To erect palaces and burying places for these rulers, man began to think about better ways of building.

Although many of those early public buildings were made of stone, most of the private houses that were built to look like them were made of wood.

An early reed house in Mesopotamia

Early cities were walled for protection.

HOUSES MADE TO LAST

Then about five thousand years ago, the first permanent houses, made of reeds from the rivers, were built in Mesopotamia, where it is believed Western civilization was born. In this area between the Tigris and Euphrates rivers in the Middle East, there were no rocks or trees available, and a building material had to be invented. Clever man looked about and decided to experiment with the mud or clay from the river banks. This material was shaped into blocks, and thus bricks came into being.

The sun-dried bricks, and later a combination of stone and brick, were used to erect the houses of the rich.

These pyramids were built in Egypt about 5,000 years ago.

This house was the home of a wealthy Egyptian family.

THE EGYPTIANS

Long ago, too, the Egyptians of northeastern Africa began to construct buildings, some of which are the oldest standing in the world today. The Egyptians were clever architects, and their pyramids, which were built as tombs for their Pharaohs, or rulers, can still be seen.

The Pharaohs lived in beautiful palaces, but the aristocratic leading citizens also had fine dwelling places. Such a home was often a one-story, courtyard structure, surrounded by a high fence. On two sides of the house, there were rooms. In the center was a garden courtyard that was half covered by roofing; this was the family's "living room."

The Egyptian aristocrat also had a country house with a garden at its center. The house was enclosed by storerooms and stables. Often, such a dwelling was quite luxurious, with a bathing room for the master, special quarters for his wife, servants' quarters, fireplaces, a kitchen, and a pool. A feature of the Egyptian house was its pillars.

Those Egyptians who were wealthy, but not of the aristocratic ruling class, lived in houses of one large room to which a smaller room was attached. The roof was flat, as it usually was in houses around the Mediterranean, and was often used for dining and sleeping.

Poor Egyptians lived in one-roomed houses that were open on one side. This room, which was used for sleeping and as a storehouse, was built of mud, brick, and reed plastered with mud. The roof was usually made of palm leaves.

HOUSES OF THE MIDDLE EAST

In the lands to the east of the Mediterranean, for example, Sumer, Babylon, Assyria, and the land of the Hebrews, the houses were similar to those of the Egyptians, with the upper classes living in two-story houses built around a court. They were "air conditioned" by watering down the walls; as the water evaporated, the building grew cooler. Houses were usually made of brick or stone and were decorated with brightly colored mats and wall hangings.

Middle class families of the Middle East lived in houses of sun-baked brick with flat roofs. Each house had several rooms. Home, for a poor family, was a one-celled hovel made of mud brick.

The home of middle-class Egyptians

An early Syrian house

THE GREEKS

One of the great cultures of all time was that of ancient Greece, which appeared not quite three thousand years ago. It had been influenced by the people of Crete, islanders who in about 2000 B.C. built palaces with drain pipes to carry away waste from baths and toilets. The Cretans were so far ahead of their time that it was not till the 1800's that Europe caught up with their plumbing system.

The houses of the rich in Greece, from 450 B.C.

to 30 B.C., were fairly modest. Women were usually restricted to the room above or behind the men's quarters. The middle class rented living space in three- or four-story tenements.

The poor of Greece lived in crude cabins, which they often shared with their animals in winter. These simple dwellings had a central hearth made of brick; the smoke escaped through a hole in the roof.

This early Greek house was built in the style of a temple.

THE ROMANS

The next stars on the stage of European history were the Romans. Legend tells us the city of Rome was founded by a man named Romulus in 750 B.C., in what is now Italy. For over a thousand years, the Romans were the most powerful people in Europe.

As great soldiers and engineers, the Romans at one time controlled a large part of modern Europe—an area extending from Turkey to England—as well as a strip of land running the entire length of the North African coast and down into Egypt as far as the Aswan Dam. They also occupied a large part of the Middle East.

We owe thanks to the Romans for many things, but especially for the alphabet we use today, and for spreading it throughout most of Europe. They were such expert builders that many examples of their work still stand. One of their most advanced engineering feats was the building of aqueducts—canals that carried fresh water from mountain streams and lakes to the cities. Sometimes these canals crossed valleys on arched bridges. Outstanding Roman aqueducts are still to be seen in France, Spain, Italy, and the Middle East.

After an aqueduct delivered it to a town, the water was carried by means of lead, terracotta, or even wooden pipes to the local fountain. From there, the people or their slaves took the water home.

A section of an aqueduct

In addition to the aqueducts, the Romans had a good sewage system. Some people who lived in private homes or in ground-floor flats had toilets, but most of the population had to pay for the use of public latrines, which were called *forciae*. All of these were flushed by water, and the sewage was then carried away in underground pipes.

ROMAN BATHS

The ancient Romans also built public baths which were often quite large and elaborate. The city of Rome had as many as seven baths at one time. One of them, the Baths of Caracalla, covered twenty-seven acres of ground, with the main building taking up six full acres. A bath might contain, in addition to a swimming pool, such things as a library, an auditorium, a steam room, a gymnasium, and a track for running. One section of the swimming pool was heated by furnaces beneath it.

THE FIRST ROMAN HOUSES

When the Latins, the founders of Rome, first arrived in Italy from Central Europe, they were simple farmers and shepherds who lived in mud huts. As Rome grew powerful enough to conquer its neighbors and spread its authority throughout Europe, the simple mud huts of Rome were replaced by more elaborate structures.

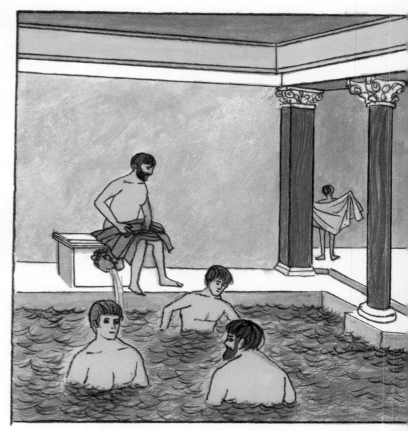

Above: Men enjoying the pool in a Roman bath

Below: Fires below the bath heated the pool and the surrounding walls.

Here is a cross section of a house of a wealthy Roman.

We have been given a fairly good idea of what Roman houses looked like because some of them are still standing just as they were in the year A.D. 79, when Mt. Vesuvius erupted and buried the city of Pompeii in Italy. The houses were preserved in the

open court. In the two-storied houses of the rich, the atrium was often ornamented and contained a garden and statues. The atrium of the middle class was smaller and sometimes roofed. Kitchens and dining areas were in the back, and the bedrooms were either on the main floor or on the second floor.

The very first Romans built houses like the one above.

ROMAN APARTMENT HOUSES

The poor folk of Rome often lived in tenement houses that were very much like the apartment houses and flats that exist today. The ground floor contained shops, and the floors above, rising sometimes as high as seven stories, were bare rooms. The height of these tenements was limited by Emperor Augustus to seventy feet—quite a height when we remember that there were no elevators in those days. But, like other houses of the time, the entire structure was built around a central court.

Many of those who lived in tenements failed to make use of Rome's good sewage system. Instead, they often threw their refuse from the windows, a custom that must have been hard on the passersby below.

lava until they were dug out within the last few hundred years.

Every house in Rome had an *atrium*, or semi-

Right: An early Roman tenement building

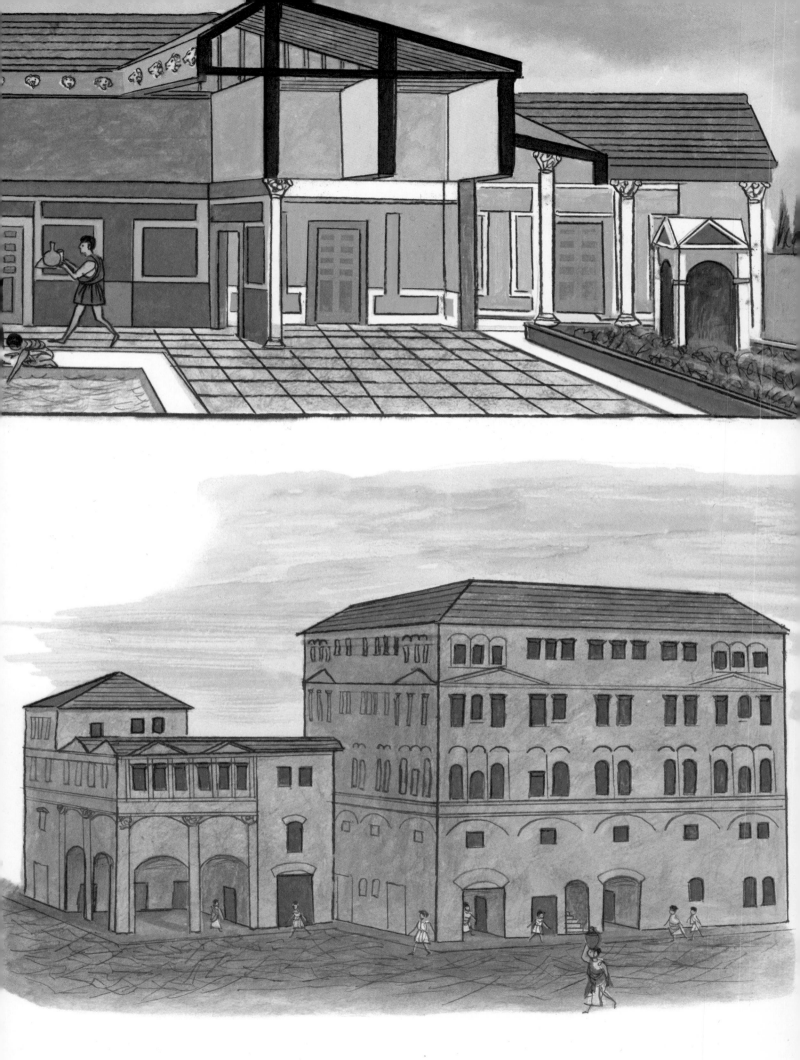

THE FEUDAL SYSTEM

By degrees, the emperors of Rome lost their power. The Roman troops were called home, although some soldiers stayed behind in lands they had grown to like.

Because those governments that remained in the western and central parts of Europe were very weak, another type of government, the *feudal system,* slowly grew to fill the need for some kind of authority. Under this system, the countryside was divided into many small communities, each one centered around a castle.

The castle was the home of a lord who ruled over the area and over the working people, called *serfs,* who lived there. The serfs farmed the land and cared for the cattle, mainly for the lord's profit. In return, when an enemy approached, the serfs fled into the castle for protection.

Until the thirteen century, the serfs themselves lived in sod huts partly dug out of the earth, or in hovels of low stone walls with thatched roofs. Unpleasant though these may seem, the dark and dirty castle in which the lord of the manor lived was not much more livable than the huts.

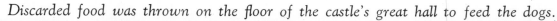

Discarded food was thrown on the floor of the castle's great hall to feed the dogs.

The Castle

The castle was mainly a place of safety, for many of the lords were constantly at war with one another. A castle was usually built on a high place so that attackers could be seen approaching. Its chief advantage was that it was highly fortified, with walls that were often several feet thick. The walls in turn were surrounded by a *moat,* a ditch filled with water. To enter the castle, the moat had to be crossed by means of a *drawbridge,* so called because when danger threatened it could be drawn up and into the castle.

Because the main reason for the castle was security, it was not often a very comfortable place. In its living room, called the *great hall,* the lord and all the people of his court lived, ate their meals, and slept. In some castles, a little grander than others, sleeping apartments were dug out of the walls for the women, but usually the people of the castle lived in the great hall; servants slept in the stables.

The Great Hall

In the thirteenth century, the great central hall was sometimes sixty feet by forty feet, with stone paving, and a hearth for a fire in the center of the room. Smoke from the fire drifted up toward the ceiling and out through a hole in the roof. Not until the beginning of the fifteenth century did the fireplace chimney come into existence.

During the Middle Ages, glass was rare, for most of it was made in Italy, and chilling drafts blew through the hall's uncovered windows. These were quite small and set high in the wall.

At one end of the great hall was a platform, called a *dais,* for meals. Behind the hall were the *buttery* where the casks of wine were kept, and the *pantry* and the *larder* where food was stored; at the other end was a *solar,* a sitting room as well as a bedroom and a private family room. The floors were covered with rushes, which were not often changed.

Half-Timber Houses

As time went on and society became more settled, people began to feel a greater need for privacy and less need for protection from their neighbors. Castle walls were still quite thick and made of brick and stone. But in the fifteenth century another type of building contruction, half-timbering, was coming into use, especially where there was little stone.

In building a half-timber house, a framework of heavy timbers was used, and the spaces between them were filled with *wattle,* an interlacing of willow or hazel branches. The wattle was then covered with *daub,* or mud.

Here is a half-timber house in Sussex, England.

The building above was a country home, but half-timber houses were also found in cities. The one below was built in the thirteenth century in the city of Rouen, France.

Many half-timber houses built in the Middle Ages are still in existence. During the heavy bombing suffered by the English people in World War II, it was a common sight to see half-timber houses withstanding the concussion of the bombs, while around them more recent brick buildings tumbled to the ground.

The houses of the middle class in the closing years of the Middle Ages were two or three stories high and had a central court for light. A front room on the ground floor was used as a shop, and behind this was the kitchen. Above the shop was a living room, and back of it were bedrooms. Some of these houses had attics. This type of house continued to be built for five hundred years.

A merchant's home near the end of the Middle Ages

The peasants' homes of the same period were surrounded by a fence, and by barns and sheds. In southern Europe, these houses were usually made of stone; wood was used in the north.

A peasant's home

CASTLES IN ENGLAND

As we have seen, castles came to Europe with the feudal system, which lasted from about the ninth century to the thirteenth century, and were built in places where lords could live in safety. But only one castle had been built in England before the eleventh century because, being an island with a stronger government, it was fairly safe from attacks from outside.

But in A.D. 1066, that strong government failed when Duke William of Normandy invaded England and defeated it. It was he, whom we now know as William the Conqueror, who made the fortified castle popular in Britain when he proceeded to erect numbers of them in all parts of the country.

William the Conqueror's structure was known in England as the "Norman" castle, although it was built like the European "Romanesque" castle. This castle and the one that followed it, the "Gothic" castle, were erected in England throughout the fifteenth century. The main difference between the Norman castle and the Gothic was that the former had round arches and the latter had pointed arches.

In the twelfth through the fifteenth centuries,

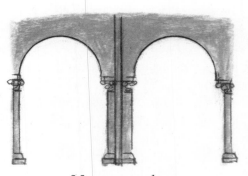

Norman arches

Gothic arches

the Gothic period, there was a good bit of traveling among European countries, especially by learned men and merchants. Because of this, the people of Europe shared architectural ideas, and the main idea of a Gothic house was the same in all lands.

The English manor house of the 15th century was a much more comfortable place to live than was the castle.

house. At first a manor house, like a castle, was often nothing more than a big hall, but as time went on such structures became roomier and more elaborate. By the fifteenth century, English manor houses differed from place to place, especially in the types of materials used. In some areas timber and plaster were used; in others, brick; some were lucky enough to be built near a quarry, and were built of stone.

The general layout of the manor house was still very much like that of the castle, but the manor house had a great many more rooms, and colorful decorations — tapestries, for example — began to appear. Carpets were imported from the East, but they were used as table coverings rather than as floor coverings. The hall was still important, but it was now used mainly at meal times and on special occasions.

A 14th-century Gothic house in Italy

THE MANOR HOUSE

By 1485, the moat had disappeared from the castle in England, and more space and attention were being given to comfortable living. The castle was no longer needed as a place of defense, and the manor house grew in importance.

A manor, as we have seen, was a large estate, and its owner or lord lived in either a castle or a manor

A great hall in a manor house

A New World Is Found

Thus far we have been looking at houses east of the Atlantic Ocean. But the sixteenth century saw bands of adventurous people from Europe crossing the Atlantic to settle in the New World.

Who was it who first discovered America? We know that Columbus landed in the Western Hemisphere in 1492, but the people of Scandinavia boast

that the Norsemen reached the Americas as early as A.D. 1000, and there are claims that the Irish arrived even before that. But the Indians had been living in the New World long before any European.

Indians in the New World

Although the Indians had been settled on the American continent for twenty thousand years, less than one million of them lived in all of North America at the time of the white man's arrival.

The Indians of North America, as we have seen, built many different kinds of shelters and houses, but all of them were quite primitive, and they had little effect on modern American housing.

It was people from Europe who gave America her homes. Settlers came from such countries as

England and France, Germany and Sweden, Spain and Italy, Holland and Denmark, and all of them brought along their habits of living—their cooking and clothing and gardens and, most important, their houses. That is why the Americas make a good workshop for people who want to know more about the buildings we call "home."

The first settlers' houses were crude indeed. Some were sod huts, and some were imitations of the Indians' wigwam. Such houses have been reconstructed at Pioneer Village in Salem, Massachusetts.

Many settlers dug pits in the ground to a depth of six or seven feet, lined them with timber, covered them with bark, and sometimes roofed them with sod. Others dug holes into a hillside and roofed them with bark. Still others built wattle-and-daub cottages, like those they had known in England and on the European continent. Houses of this type have been reconstructed at Jamestown, Virginia.

Houses in New England

After the early settlers were really settled in the new land, they built more permanent dwellings. The early houses of New England were copies of the medieval house of England, but because the climate of New England was much harsher than that of England, certain changes had to be made. For one thing, the snow storms of New England were heavier than those in the mother country, and so the roofs were steeply pitched, coming almost to the ground in some cases. The roof was then covered with tightly packed thatches of straw. A pitched roof also helped to keep the inside of the house warm.

The windows of these houses were small, and because the heat could escape through them, they were few in number. Although some windows were made of glass, this material was scarce, and most of them were covered with oiled paper which the colonists had brought from England.

A salt box house had a roof that was deeper at the back than at the front.

The houses were built of wood for two reasons. First, the great forests of the New World provided plenty of wood. The second reason was a belief that a house built of wood was healthy.

Salt Box Houses

Some early American dwellings, called salt box houses, had only one room, but most of them had two rooms on the first floor; winding stairs led to two rooms above. Across one end of the main room was a large chimney stack made of a wooden frame packed with clay. This frame, together with the thatch of the roof, was a fire hazard, and great care had to be taken lest the fire escape up the framework and onto the thatched roof.

The main room of the house was called the *hall*. It was there that the family ate its meals, the women did their spinning, and the men did many of their various small chores. There, too, meals were cooked in the fireplace, which also gave light and heat.

The second room on the main floor was sometimes a parlor, but sometimes it was also a workroom or a bedroom.

On the upper floors were bedrooms, and often there was more than one bed in each. Children seldom had a bed to themselves, for they had to share with brothers and sisters.

Of course, there wasn't much furniture in the houses of the early settlers. It was made by hand and was quite plain, for men were too busy to spend time decorating chairs and tables. Near the fireplace, there might be a few stools and benches, and a table. Possibly there might also be a settle (a long bench with a high back and arms), a spinning wheel, a loom to make cloth, and of course beds.

The latter were either four-posters or jackbeds. Jackbeds were part of a house; they were built into a corner with the walls of the corner forming two sides of the bed. Mattresses were stuffed with feathers, straws, or rags. All these houses had chests for storing tools, utensils, and clothing.

The Cape Cod cottage was built low as a protection against the heavy winds.

CAPE COD COTTAGES

While the salt box house was being built in southern New England, another type of house was being built on Cape Cod, in Massachusetts. This house—the Cape Cod cottage—was made of wood from the nearby forests.

The outside was either clapboard or wood shingle. Like the salt box house, the Cape Cod cottage was planned around the central chimney.

In colonial Virginia, many houses had two chimneys.

At the end of a hard day's work on the farm or on a fishing boat, parents and children gathered in the big kitchen at the back of the house. The other rooms on the first floor—the parlor and the bedrooms—were smaller than the kitchen.

BRICK HOUSES IN VIRGINIA

In Virginia, the first settlers, who were also from England, built houses like those in Massachusetts. These medieval-looking houses were also made of wood with timber frames, and had wood and clay chimneys and clapboard sidings. However, probably because the climate was damp, these buildings did not stand up well, and before long the Virginians began to build houses of brick.

In New England, a vestibule inside the front door kept cold winds from blowing through the house when the door was opened. But in warmer Virginia, the front door was likely to open onto one of the rooms. In many Virginian houses, a central hall went from the front of the house to the back, with rooms opening from the hall on either side. The poorer folk of Virginia lived in simple one- and two-room layouts with leantos for additions.

SPANISH HOUSES IN FLORIDA

The oldest house in what is now the United States was probably built in 1571 by the Spanish in St. Augustine, Florida, which had been settled in 1565. This structure, with its Spanish style porches and a balcony overlooking a patio that contained a garden, served as a home and chapel for monks who had arrived with the settlers.

THE DUTCH IN THE NEW WORLD

At the beginning of the seventeenth century, the greatest commercial people in world were the Dutch. They had many more ships at sea than any other nation. Some Dutch merchants decided at that time to set up trading posts near the site of Albany, on the Hudson River, and on Manhattan Island.

In 1623, other Dutch families made their homes on Manhattan Island, Long Island, and in New Jersey, opposite the present city of Philadelphia. Later, all the land settled by the Dutch was claimed by England, for an Italian explorer named Cabot had sailed the length of the Atlantic coast under the English flag. Thus, in 1664, the Dutch governor,

Peter Stuyvesant, gave up the city of Nieuw Amsterdam to the English, and it became New York.

DUTCH HOUSES

The first Dutch colonists built crude shelters, but they soon began to erect dwellings modeled on those at home in Holland. Their first permanent buildings were frame houses, but having been the best brickmakers in Europe, they built kilns for baking brick in about 1630. Soon they were erecting brick houses like those in the homeland.

Following the Dutch style, some of their houses were four or five stories high; this made them the highest homes in the New World. The owner of such a house might have a shop on the ground floor and live with his family in the rooms above.

The Dutch also built houses along the Hudson Valley, and in parts of New Jersey, on Long Island, and in what is now Brooklyn and a part of New York City. The first stone houses were made from field stone that was laid evenly for all four walls. The walls were then packed with clay.

Another feature of these houses was the *stoop*, a small planked platform at the front door. Two benches, one on either side of the door, faced each other across the stoop. In later houses, the projecting roof in the front got bigger and bigger, and eventually supports were necessary to hold it up. Of course, as the projection got larger, so also did the stoop underneath, until finally it ran the entire length of the front of the house and became a full front porch.

The Dutch were very neat people, and even though there were beds in these houses, they were built in against the walls or in alcoves, and during the day they were covered with draperies.

THE LOG CABIN

The Swedes, too, contributed to early American housing with the log cabin, which became an important part of many pioneer settlements. There is evidence that log houses were being built in Scandinavia as early as A.D. 300. All of those early dwellings have long since crumbled away, but one *laftehus* (the log cabin's Norwegian name), built in 1250, can still be seen in a museum in Oslo. In the five hundred years that followed the building of that *laftehus*, few changes were made in its basic plan. Wooden floors, windows, and fireplaces were added, but the appearance changed little.

The gambrel roof, with two slopes on either side, was the mark of many a Dutch colonial house.

In 1638, the Swedes established a settlement along the Delaware River where the city of Wilmington now stands. It was called Fort Christiana. Being more used to the forest than settlers from other parts of Europe, the Swedes cleared the land of trees, and with them built log cabins.

Other settlers saw that the log cabin was an excellent house for the wilderness, and as greater numbers of people pushed into the New World, they imitated the Swedes by building more log cabins.

The log cabin, brought to America by the Swedes, was used by pioneers in the West.

In different places, different materials were used in building the Georgian house.

Later in the seventeenth century, others came to North America, including the Scotch, the Irish, and the Germans. Their settlement succeeded, and the new colonists built houses that were like those already standing.

A QUAKER SETTLEMENT

A particularly successful settlement was that of the Quakers at Philadelphia under William Penn. As these people prospered, they built some magnificent houses which were also imitations of a building style then used by other colonies. It was called *Georgian* after the four English kings of the eighteenth century, all of whom were named George.

THE FRENCH AND SPANISH IN AMERICA

Although the French and Spanish were important explorers of the North American continent, they did very little colonizing. The Spanish made some attempts to settle in Florida and the Southwest, but these efforts were made mostly by missionaries.

The early Spanish missions in what is now the southwestern United States were made of thatch, but before long the missionaries began to copy the Indians' homes in that area by building houses of adobe, or of stone and adobe. The Spanish buildings were different from those of the Indians in that the Spaniards used wood for the frames of doors and windows.

The missionaries arranged their buildings around an open court or patio and used clay tiles for their roofs. Both of these ideas were Spanish.

Although the Spaniards never settled the Southwest in any great numbers, some towns and villages did spring up around the missions. The houses in these towns resembled the mission buildings.

THE FIRST RANCH HOUSES

As ranching developed in the Southwest, the first ranch houses seem to have been part Indian and part Spanish in style. Made of sun-dried brick, they were covered with plaster and then whitewashed.

Such houses were built around three sides of a patio and were usually of one story. The roof was flat with projecting beams like those of the Indian pueblo. The roof of the walls facing the patio was often extended over the patio and supported with beams to make a shady and fairly cool veranda. In some of the houses of more than one story, the upper floor was reached by an outside stairway.

FRENCH HOUSES IN THE NEW WORLD

In 1608, a French community was established at Quebec in Canada. The first houses were crude and primitive, with stone foundations and chimneys, and wooden walls. After a time, much of the architecture began to look like that of a part of France called Normandy, from which the settlers had come. A house of this type was one and a half stories high with a very steep roof which projected beyond the supporting walls; the purpose of this was to help keep the snow from piling up too high. There were few windows because the Canadian winters were cold and long, and the snows were heavy. These houses were so well suited to Quebec's climate that houses like them are still being built there.

In 1720, the site of New Orleans, part of the French territory of Louisiana and located at the mouth of the Mississippi River, was divided into a hundred squares and then into sixty-foot lots. This small section still exists today and is known as the *French Quarter*. The first settlers there built houses of beams of cypress, a wood native to that area. The roofs were palmetto thatch. The walls were made of soft bricks that were molded from Mississippi River sand.

In buildings of one and a half stories, the front rooms that opened onto the street were shops, and the living quarters were either behind the shop or in the upper story. Because of the hot, rainy climate, the steep roofs projected far beyond the walls.

The Alamo, a famous example of Spanish building in the United States

Here is an early French building in the mid-western United States.

27

Houses in Europe

We have looked at the early houses in the New World because in that vast and empty land a house had to be built for every colonist. We have seen how many of the countries of Europe that founded colonies in various parts of the continent built houses like those at home.

Here is a tall timber-framed house built in London, England, at about the time the first colonies were being settled in the New World.

In Europe, of course, changes in the styles of housing were still going on. In England, gradual changes in earlier castles led to the development of the manor house, while in France, similar changes saw the growth of the chateau. Here is one of these homes of the rich that was built in France at the time of the settlement of the New World. It is called Vaux-le-Vicomte, and was started in 1656.

This is an eighteenth century stone cottage from Cambridgeshire, England.

At that time, the house of a wealthy Italian family looked like this.

In parts of Switzerland houses with straw roofs looked like this.

A 17th century London street

In the middle of the eighteenth century, the first Swiss chalets appeared.

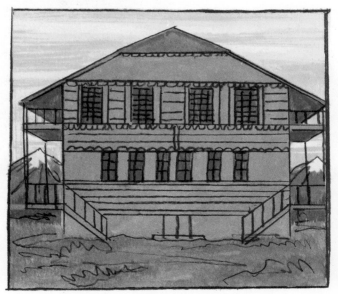

A Danish town house of the same period might have looked like this.

Toward the end of the eighteenth century, some Danish country houses looked like this.

This house from Somerset, England, dates from 1720.

29

LIFE IN THE NEW WORLD COLONIES

During the colonial period in North America, most communities, particularly along the Atlantic coast, were settled by the British, and their architecture was strongly influenced by England. After the American Revolution, the new nation began to turn its back on English influence and toward continental Europe for models.

The colonial period also saw the beginnings of the Industrial Revolution, an era in which new inventions completely changed the way of life in Europe and America. Before this time, people had traveled from city to city in horse-drawn stage-coaches or similar vehicles. Families got their heat from fireplaces and their light from candles. Farm tools and farming methods had not changed in hundreds of years. Women spun animals' fleeces into yarn on spinning wheels at home, and then wove the yarn into cloth on looms.

19TH-CENTURY INVENTIONS

Then a series of discoveries and inventions began to make life easier.

By the early nineteenth century, people were able to travel from place to place by train or by steamships.

In the home, fireplaces gave way to cast-iron stoves, and oil lamps replaced candles.

Farming methods were improved by the iron plow, and mills began to weave cloth by machine. Factories produced iron tools and utensils.

These improvements reduced the need for farm workers, and many people flocked to the cities to take jobs in factories. As a result, the cities became overcrowded and disease began to spread, mainly because of poor plumbing.

THE STORY OF PLUMBING

At the end of the sixteenth century, a Sir John Harrington of England had invented a water closet, or toilet, that could be flushed by water, but people were not interested in it. Later, a man named Alexander Cummings, in 1755, and a Joseph Bramah, in 1778, patented flush toilets in England, but their inventions were quite expensive and so difficult to keep clean that people didn't want to be bothered with them.

Aside from such false starts, very little had been done to improve plumbing since the building of the Roman aqueducts. Then, in the nineteenth century, separate systems for water supply and for sewage were introduced for the first time. Plumbing fixtures were developed, and water closets, or flush toilets, as well as bathtubs and lavatories, began to appear.

Throughout the centuries, lighting came in many shapes.

Even though the waste pipes were underground, sewer gases and vermin from sewers still infected houses, but with the introduction of the sanitary trap in the latter half of the nineteenth century, this problem was solved. Still, many houses in country places went on using wells as a source of water.

New Ways of Lighting

Improvements in lighting also took place during the nineteenth century. Up until that time, light came from a flame that was produced by either candles or oil lamps. Despite the fact that centuries before the birth of Christ, natural gas had been used in China, it was not used in the Western world till the latter part of the eighteenth century. In 1806, gas was introduced in the United States when it was used for street lighting. The first indoor use was in Philadelphia in 1816. But this gas flame gave a flickering, unsteady light until a German scientist named Von Welsbach invented a gas mantle in 1885. This could be placed over the naked flame, which then glowed as steadily as our present-day electric bulbs.

The Electric Bulb

The electric bulb was invented in 1879 by Thomas Edison, an American, but a great deal of pioneering work by scientists in many countries had made Edison's work possible, as you will read on pages 56 and 57 of this book.

In the second half of the nineteenth century, many useful inventions began to appear on the market. Among them were such helps to business and daily life as the bicycle, the microphone, the cable car, the typewriter, and the telephone.

American Gothic

Great numbers of people were needed to make the new inventions. Thus more jobs became available, and people had more money to spend. To display their new wealth, many families built houses that were pretentious and highly decorated. In the United States, many of these were built in what was called the *American Gothic* style, an imitation of the Gothic castles of England. At first such houses were built only by wealthy folk, but before long they

An American Gothic house

An example of Carpenters' Gothic

were being copied by those in the middle class and by poorer people, too.

When the bandsaw was invented, carpenters were able to cut a great variety of intricate designs from wood. Some of the more modest houses had decorations around the eaves, above the doors, and along the edges of the roofs, all made by the bandsaw. Such houses came to be known as *Carpenters' Gothic*.

ITALIAN VILLAS

Another type of house that influenced architecture in North America at this time was the Italian villa. One feature of many such villas in America was the square tower. Others had a cube-shaped lookout on top of a flat roof. This lookout was called a *cupola*, an *observatory*, or a *belvedere*, depending on the part of the country in which the

house was located. Although most of these villas were built of stone, many were made of wood. In the cities, the Italian influence can still be seen in some of the buildings called *brownstones*.

THE MANSARD ROOF

The third important influence in the second half of the nineteenth century came from France. This was the *mansard* roof, which had been invented two hundred years before by a French architect named Francois Mansart.

A mansard roof had four steep sides into which larger dormer windows were placed. In a house with a roof of this type, the attic space could be used for living quarters. If you have ever been inside the attic of a house with a very steep, pitched roof, you know how cramped it can be. Indeed, in a large part of such an attic one cannot walk upright.

A house with a mansard roof

A square tower atop an Italian villa

This is not true of a house with a mansard roof. The attic rooms are quite comfortable, although slightly smaller than the rooms on the floors below.

Mansard homes were built in cities, in small towns and villages, and on farms. They were constructed of wood, brick, and many kinds of stone.

Cast-Iron Buildings

An interesting structure from this period—the second half of the nineteenth century—was the cast-iron building. In England, builders had started to use cast iron as a building material late in the eighteenth century. The French picked it up around 1840, and several famous buildings in Paris were made of it. What is perhaps the most famous cast-iron structure in the world was built in Paris in 1889; this is the Eiffel Tower, which has become a symbol for Paris.

The iron buildings of the latter nineteenth century were prefabricated, that is, parts of them came ready to be put into place without further work. Great claims were made for such structures. They were supposed to be superior to other kinds of buildings in resisting strain.

But cast-iron buildings had their shortcomings, too. They were expensive to build and had to be painted frequently to prevent rust. The worst flaw of such buildings came to light in 1871 during the Great Fire in Chicago. Because the metal could not withstand the intense heat, many of the city's cast-iron buildings collapsed before the flames touched them. This put an end to iron buildings.

Buildings Grow Taller

Because of the great numbers of people crowding into the cities in the second half of the nineteenth century, they went on spreading farther and farther from the center. Then two things happened that helped cities to grow upward rather than outward.

Before this time, each floor of a building had to be supported by the floor beneath it. This meant that the higher a building went, the stronger the lowest floors had to be. Of course, this put a limit on how tall a structure could be.

A second restriction on the height of buildings was a more human one. There weren't many people who wanted to walk up more than four or five flights of stairs. Although some apartment houses were built with as many as seven stories, the upper floors of high buildings were hard to rent.

The first of these problems was solved when

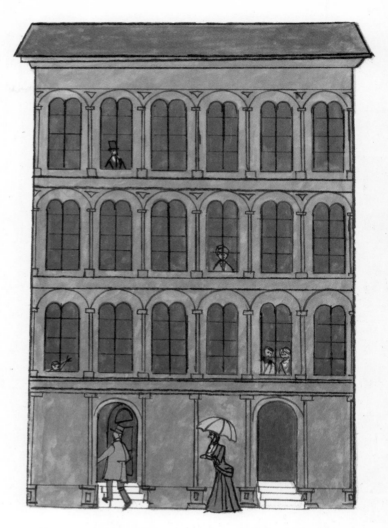

Cast-iron buildings like the one above were thought to be safe in thunderstorms.

steel frames were used for new buildings. The second was solved when an American inventor named Elisha Otis invented a contraption called an *elevator* in 1852.

Elevators made tall buildings possible.

Built in 1884, the Home Insurance Building in Chicago was the first skyscraper.

THE SKYSCRAPER

In 1884, the first skyscraper with a steel skeleton frame was built in Chicago. It was a success, and after that more and more skyscrapers began to appear in large American cities. A really big one was the sixty-story Woolworth Building, completed in New York in 1913.

For many years, the 102-story Empire State Building, also in New York, was the tallest skyscraper in the world. However, the recently completed 110-story World Trade Center, another New York building, now holds the title.

APARTMENT HOUSES

As we have seen, apartment buildings have a long history, going back to Roman times. In Europe, where many cities were surrounded by walls to keep out invaders, the cities could not spread out. Instead, they had to move upward, and apartment buildings became a common part of city life.

In New York, the first such building was the Stuyvesant Apartment, built in 1869. It was a five-story brick structure. Since it had no elevator, it was called a *walk-up*.

After the steel skeleton and the elevator came into common use, a building could be almost as high as its planner wished. Unfortunately, many tall apartments were not handsome or pleasant to live in. Many of those erected at the beginning of the twentieth century were monotonous, both inside and out. Often the only thing a tenant saw from the window of such an apartment was another apartment across the way.

Apartment buildings are now usually designed to look like a T or an X when viewed from above. In such buildings, every apartment has a view of the outside, and no two apartments face each other.

The apartments being built today are equipped to make life as comfortable as possible. Each one may have its own incinerator, garbage disposal unit, washer and dryer, and air conditioner. Some are built on grounds that provide for their tenants such features as swimming pools, tennis courts, and golf courses. All the new apartments have garage space for tenants' cars right in the building.

EARLY 20TH-CENTURY LIFE

Although life was becoming easier, the average person at the beginning of the twentieth century

was still not enjoying the inventions of the nineteenth century. Installing plumbing and electric and telephone lines was expensive and took a great deal of time. It would be some years before people in the country, and city people who did not have much money, would have the comfort of the new inventions.

THE TELEPHONE

Telephones, which up till that time had been used mostly in business offices and institutions, were beginning to take their place in the home. But they were not like the phones we know today. On each one there was a little crank that had to be turned to get the operator's attention. Usually there were four or more families on each line, and often a caller had to wait some time before his turn came.

To make things worse, all the people on a line could listen to the conversations of all the others on the same line! It wasn't wise to discuss secrets on the phone in those days.

Another improvement that was making life pleasanter was Thomas Edison's electric lights, which were beginning to be seen in homes. But most houses were still lighted by gas or oil lamps.

CENTRAL HEATING

Central heating, a method that used one central source to heat many rooms or even a whole house, was growing more common. It was a great improvement over the fireplace or stove that heated only one room. In the early central heating systems, furnaces were located in the basement and usually heated the first floor only. Most of them were coal-burning, hot-air furnaces.

Water for the bath was heated on the stove.

INDOOR PLUMBING

Most houses still did not have indoor plumbing. The toilet was located in a little shed called a *privy*, behind the house. There was a steel kitchen sink into which water flowed from a hand pump.

Bathrooms were not yet common, and baths were often taken in the kitchen, the one really warm room in the house. Where central heating was still not in use, the kitchen's heat came from a large, black, cast-iron stove that usually burned wood, although some such stoves burned coal. On this stove, too, was done all the cooking and baking for the household.

Women still washed their clothes in large tubs, with scrubbing boards, coarse brushes, and bars of strong soap. The laundry had to be hung to dry in the yard or on the apartment-house roof.

RADIOS AND PHONOGRAPHS

In the early years of the twentieth century, radios called *crystal sets*, that is, sets without vacuum tubes, began to appear. Instead of speakers, head phones were used. The phonograph, which used cylindrical records, began to be popular, and people were able to listen to raspy recordings of such singers as Enrico Caruso, a great tenor of the day.

THE NEW WORLD GROWS

At the beginning of the twentieth century, populations began to increase even more rapidly than in the previous century. This was especially true in the United States, where great waves of immigrants arrived from Europe. As the number of people grew larger, the need for new homes became pressing. In the United States alone, the number of new houses built in a single year grew from 200,000 in 1900 to over 2,000,000 in 1972.

The three very different houses above were built in the 20th century.

If we were to drive through the outskirts of any large city to look at the new housing developments, we might think they all looked alike. This might be true of the houses in any one development, but the houses vary from one section to another.

BUILDERS' NEEDS DON'T CHANGE!

In the early part of this book, we looked at the things that were important to a builder in the early history of man. These are just as important today in places where the homes of Europe and America would not be suitable. Among them are the *materials at hand*. A native of a village in Central Africa, wishing to build an igloo, would find it impossible, for where would he get the ice? Even if he were to build an igloo, it wouldn't suit his purpose, for it was designed to withstand the bitter climate of the frozen North. But what our native really wants is a house that would be fairly cool in Central Africa's oppressive heat.

This illustrates the second thing that is important in building a house: *the climate in which it is to be erected.*

A third factor is the *life style* of the people who will live in the house. If, on open land in a large city, such as New York, London, Rome, or Paris, someone were to put up an Indian tepee as his home, he would be regarded as a bit peculiar. But also, should a member of the nomadic tribes of the African desert build himself a brick house with all modern conveniences, he too would be considered strange. The nomadic tribes are constantly on the move and must carry their houses with them. A brick house would not do at all.

In parts of Africa, South America, Hawaii and other islands of the Pacific, the people still build simple huts of thatch. The thatch is often made from grasses or bamboo, as well as from the leaves of banana or palm trees.

The hut below is from Samoa and has no walls. Blinds can be raised or lowered on the sides, mainly to keep out the weather. Although the hut looks fragile, it has lived through many hurricanes.

The Dorze people of Ethiopia are expert weavers, and much of their weaving goes into the making of their bamboo huts. These have a projection over the entrance to keep out the rain. As we have seen, a house built in this shape is called a beehive hut.

Here is a house from New Britain, an island in the Pacific near Australia. Its walls are made of hand-hewn planks, and the roof of thatch.

The houses of the Masakin tribe in the Sudan of Africa look very much like medieval castles on a small scale. The hut walls are of mud, and the roof is made of thatch.

In one of the circular rooms, the parents sleep; another houses the animals; and upstairs is a loft for the children. The remaining rooms are work and storage areas. In the enclosed court yard, the cooking is done.

Members of the Higaonon tribe of the Philippines live in treehouses, and one of these may have as many as fifty tenants. The tree houses were originally built as a defense against hostile tribes.

These unusual looking houses are from one of the Indonesian islands. Their shiplike appearance has led some anthropologists to speculate that at one time the people who built them may have been sailors. The roofs of these houses are made of bamboo; the walls are often highly decorated.

Here is a house in Burma, a country of Southeast Asia. It is cooled by air which enters the house through walls made of bamboo that has been woven like a basket. Such an air-cooled house is well suited to Burma's very hot climate.

Anatolian farmers of Turkey live in the houses shown below. The cone-shaped rocks are of volcanic origin. Monks, many centuries ago, dug retreats into the soft material of the cones, and some present-day farmers have taken these retreats as their homes. Occasionally, new homes are fashioned here in the style of the originals. People enter a house by means of a ladder.

In some parts of the world, people build their houses on stilts to keep out snakes, insects, and other animals. The houses below are in New Guinea.

The Bushmen of the Kalahari in southern Africa use these grass shelters, which are called *skerms*. One of them can be built by the women of the tribe in less than an hour. Usually, a skerm provides a place for storing tools and other possessions, for Bushmen prefer to sleep outdoors.

In areas near bodies of water, such as this one in Indonesia, houses are often built on piles, to avoid flooding.

This Japanese house now stands in Philadelphia; a Japanese garden surrounds it.

JAPANESE HOUSES

In Japan, the traditional house is made from wood and paper. Unlike our dwellings, many Japanese houses have no doors or windows. Two, and sometimes three, of its outer walls are often movable, being made of *shoji,* or sliding screens.

The screens are covered with rice paper that allows light to enter the house. The fourth, or permanent wall, is of unpainted wood, or of wood painted black. Occasionally it is plastered, in which case the plaster is either white or dark slate in color.

The partitions in the interior of this house are also screens that run along grooves in the floor and ceiling. These screens can be put in place to form a room, or pushed aside to enlarge it.

We have already read about the tepee, the house of the American Indians that could be picked up and put down in another place. In some parts of the world people are still living in movable houses. There are sections of China where people are born and raised on boats and never know any other home until the day they die. In some Chinese cities, as much as a quarter of the population lives in houseboats.

MOVABLE HOUSES

Nomads, of course, also live in movable houses. We spoke earlier of the nomadic Bedouins of the Sahara Desert who live in tents made of goat hair. The Bedouin has followed his herds of goats across the desert for centuries. Although he is always careful to find adequate water for his animals, he seldom drinks it himself. Instead, he drinks the milk of his goats.

In Mongolia, other goat herders live in round portable huts called *gors* or *yurts*. These are covered with felt and have stoves inside. They can withstand temperatures as low as — 50° Fahrenheit. Today many yurts are made in factories; sometimes they are even set up in cities as permanent residences. A yurt always faces south so that the cold northern wind can not blow through the door opening.

One nomadic people whom many of us know are the gypsies, who were believed to have come originally from India and to have wandered through

Asia and into Europe. Because they claimed to have come from Egypt, they were called *gypsies*. Traditionally, the gypsy bought and sold horses, but with the coming of the automobile, this trade was no longer profitable. Today many gypsies deal in automobiles.

All these people are just as comfortable in their homes as we are in our very special house.

How Your House Works

We have looked at many houses. Some were very simple, such as the caves of earliest man and the grass huts of today's African Bushmen. Some were grander and more impressive, such as the villas of ancient Rome, the castles of medieval Europe, and the manor houses of England. But none of these houses were as comfortable and convenient as the house you live in now.

There are three things that set the modern western house apart from those of other times and other parts of the world: running water and plumbing, electricity, and the central heating system.

Today, if you are thirsty, you turn the cold faucet, and out pours good clean water. If a member of your family wants to wash clothes, he puts them into the washing machine, turns on the water, adds the detergent, and lets the machine do the laundry.

Washing by electricity is quite uncommon—even unknown—in many parts of the world. In some places, to this day, women carry the clothes

to be washed down to a stream, where they scrub each article by hand, one at a time. In other places, women do their washing at the village fountain.

In some primitive areas water, which we need to live, must be carried home in jugs from rivers and streams. In other places, even in some parts of Europe and North America, people still dig wells to find water. In some wells, a bucket full of water is raised from the well by means of a crank called a *windlass*. In others, the water is pumped up by electricity.

Fire was a constant danger in the days of oil lamps and candles, wooden houses, thatched roofs, and open fireplaces, and people helped one another to put them out. In early colonial times in America, fire brigades fought fires by passing buckets of water along a line of people that stretched from a river or stream to the fire. A second line passed the empty buckets from the fire to the stream to be refilled.

40

41

"WATER SEEKS ITS OWN LEVEL"

Rivers and streams flow in only one direction —from a higher place to a lower one. Towns and cities take advantage of this fact by constructing streets in such a way that the center of the road is higher than the gutters. When the rain comes, it must flow from the high center of the road into the gutters. These are also graded so that the water flows down from them into a grating that opens into the sewer. If you were to follow this water further, you would find that the underground pipes are also slanted downward so that the water continues to flow.

If all water flows downward, how is it that we can turn on a faucet on the second or third floor and have water come out of it? After all, we know that water from the city pipes enters the house at the cellar level. Does the water flow up? As a matter of fact, in our houses the water does flow up! How can this be?

AN EXPERIMENT

Try this experiment. You will need two empty milk cartons and a length of rubber hose about two feet long. On one side and near the bottom

of each carton, make a hole with the end of a pencil. You are going to squeeze one end of the hose into each hole, so be careful to make the holes just large enough and no larger. A good way to do this is to put the small end of a flared toothpaste cap into each hole. Then, turning slowly, enlarge the holes to the proper size.

Take one end of the hose and squeeze it into the hole at the bottom of carton A. Then put the other end of the hose through the hole in carton B. You should now have something that looks like this.

Next take the two milk cartons and place them in a sink. Fill half of carton A with water. What happens? The water flows from carton A through the hose at the bottom into carton B, and both cartons end up holding the same amount of water.

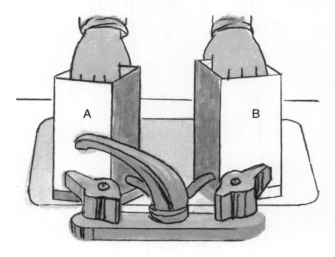

If you fill carton A to the top, you will see that the water in it soon decreases. At the same time the water will have risen in carton B. Each carton will be about half full.

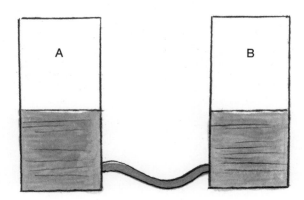

This experiment shows that water always seeks its own level. The only way you could keep carton A filled, would be to fill carton B.

Now take carton A and place it on the drainboard. Place carton B in the bowl of the sink.

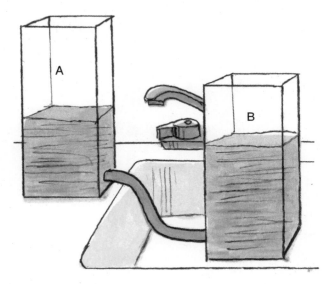

What happens? The water in carton A begins to go down, and the water in carton B rises. The water in carton B will continue to rise until it is at exactly the same level as the water in carton A.

What is happening? The water is entering carton B at the bottom and is actually rising in it in order to reach the same level as the water in carton A.

Now empty the water from both cartons. Remove the hose from the bottom of carton B. Put your finger in the end of the hose and fill half of carton A with water. Put the other end of the hose into the sink and remove your finger. The water flows out of the hose.

Now pick up the hose and carry it higher and higher over the sink. The water continues to flow from the hose only until it reaches the water level in carton A. It will not flow above this level. If you want the water to flow again, you must lower the hose below this point.

Put the hose back in the bowl of the sink, and plug it with your finger or a piece of cork.

There is still water in carton A, but since the hose has been plugged, nothing is coming out of it. This is the condition that exists in your house when all the faucets are turned off. Your finger or the cork represents the faucet in the system that keeps the water from flowing. But the pressure that makes it flow is still there. Remove the cork. The water flows. Replace the cork, and the water stops.

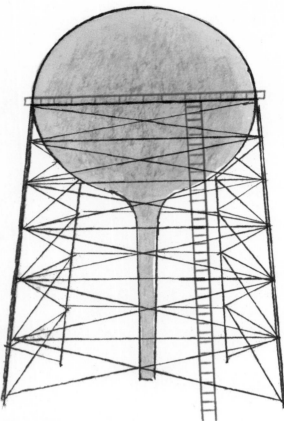

THE STANDPIPE

If you live in a city, your water comes from the local water system. First, water for the city is collected in a reservoir. Sometimes this is done by building a dam across a river, causing a large lake, or reservoir, to be formed. The water in the lake is then piped to the city. Sometimes reservoirs are several hundred miles from the city they service. Other cities may get their water from a mountain lake nearby. Still others, which are located on a body of fresh water such as a river or lake, might use this local source for their water supply. This local water would first have to go through a purification plant to make it clean enough to drink.

When the water is ready to be used for the people of a city, it must come from a place that is higher than any of the buildings that are to use it. To cities that get their water from high mountain streams or lakes, this is no problem, for their source of supply is already high. But in cities where this is not the case, the water must be pumped to a higher place.

Sometimes the water is pumped into a standpipe —a large tank located in a higher position than any of the buildings to be serviced. But why is it necessary to use a standpipe when the water must be pumped up to it in the first place? The answer is this: If the water were to be pumped directly into the buildings, it would tend to pulsate as it came from the faucet.

To see why this happens, again put the milk carton in the sink. Half fill it with water, keeping your finger over the end of the hose.

Now, placing the carton under the faucet, rapidly turn the faucet on and off so that the water comes in spurts. Remove your finger from the

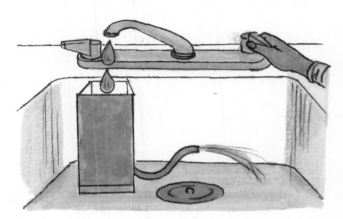

hose, and continue to turn the faucet on and off. You will notice that, although the water goes into the carton in spurts, it comes out of the end of the hose in an even flow.

That is what happens in a standpipe. The pressure inside the tank from the water keeps it flowing at an even rate in all the buildings.

THE FAUCET

All faucets do not look alike. Some have the "off-on" handle on the top, as in most sinks, and others have this handle on the side, as in a shower. But all of them operate in the same way.

Here is what happens.

The piece of metal on which the handle is attached is called the stem. At the end of the stem is a washer, made of rubber or plastic.

When you turn off the faucet, you screw down the stem at the same time to make the plastic washer sit snugly on the *seat*, a part of the faucet at the bottom. When the stem is in this "off" position, the flow of water is blocked.

If the handle is turned in the opposite direction, the stem is screwed away from the seat. This unblocks the water and it flows into the sink.

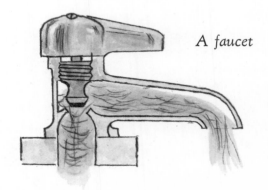

A faucet

THE TOILET TANK

Shut-off valves in such appliances as washing machines and dish washers, as well as the valve in the toilet tank, operate on the same principle.

Here is how the toilet tank works:

First remove the lid from the tank, being careful not to drop it, and flush the toilet. As you do this, a long arm attached to the handle inside the tank lifts a piece of metal about the size of a thick wire. This piece of metal controls, in turn, a similar piece having a rubber stopper on its other end. The rubber stopper sits over a large hole at the bottom of the tank. The handle arm lifts the first piece of metal, which raises the stopper so the water can flow out of the large hole in the bottom of the tank and into the toilet.

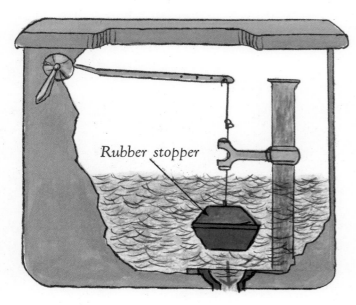

Rubber stopper

Gradually, as the water in the tank decreases, the rubber stopper, which is held in position over the hole, begins to float down and is sucked into the hole. Thus the water is stopped from flowing out of the tank.

A pipe enters the bottom of the tank, as you can see at the top of column 2. This is the water supply. At the top of this pipe there is a valve. Attached to it is a long rod with a large, round, hollow metal or plastic ball on its end.

When the toilet is flushed, the ball, which floats on the water, flops down as the water recedes. When this happens, the position of the rod attached to the ball changes, opening the valve so the water can flow into the tank.

Gradually, as the tank fills with water, the ball changes the position of the rod. When the ball rises to a certain level, the position of the rod turns off the valve, and the water stops flowing.

It will stay in this position until the next time the toilet is flushed.

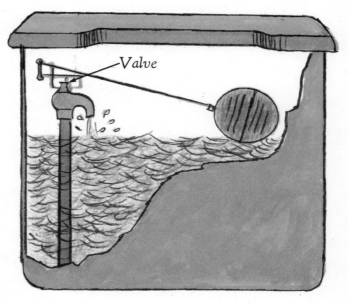

Valve

You know now how the water gets into the system. What happens when it leaves the sink? When you remove the stopper, the water goes down the drain by force of gravity. If you look at the drainpipe under the sink you will notice that it curves first up and then down. Why is this?

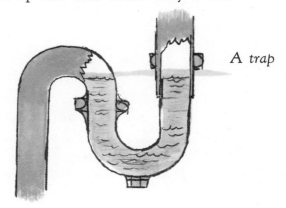

A trap

THE DRAINAGE SYSTEM

All drains connect directly with the waste pipe in the basement; the waste pipe, in turn, connects with sewer pipes under the street. What is to prevent all of the odors from the sewer pipes from coming back through the wastepipe and into the house? It is those curved pipes under the sink.

When water goes into the drain in a sink, it washes down and up the curved pipe and into the the waste pipe in the basement. But the last little bit of water that goes into the drain can not, because of gravity, push its way up to the top curve in the pipe under the sink.

Remember that when the last water in the drain reaches the bottom of this curved pipe, it

45

stops flowing. This water then stays where it is at the bottom of the curved pipe and no odor can get past it and into the room. The curved pipe has trapped the odor and so, it is called a trap.

The water will sit in the trap until the sink is used again. At that time, the water is pushed up and into the waste pipe, while other water takes its place.

After the water leaves the drain of the sink, it flows down a large vertical pipe called the *stack*. This pipe connects in the basement with the main waste pipe. The waste pipe is slanted slightly downward, carrying the wastes into the sewer under the street. The sewer pipes are also slanted, permitting the wastes to move on to the disposal plant.

THE WATER SUPPLY

Go down into your basement. Somewhere on the wall nearest the street, you will find a pipe coming through the wall. It should feel cold to the touch. This pipe, which is usually not more than an inch and a half in diameter, is the house water supply, coming directly from the city water mains. In many cities, it is connected with a meter that measures the amount of water you use.

Soon after leaving the meter, the supply pipe will enter a valve which operates in the same way as a faucet. When this valve is turned on you have water in the house. When it is turned off there is no water, and so it is called the main valve.

Near the valve there should be a spigot outlet. This allows the plumber, after he has turned off the water at the main valve, to remove all water left in the pipes of the house. This must be done if he is to make his repairs. It is especially important when he is working with copper tubing, for he must heat the various joints in order to melt the solder used to seal the joints. If water were inside the pipes, it would be impossible to get the metal hot enough for melting to take place.

Here water enters the house.

The waste pipe

The stack

The furnace

46

After you have shut off the main valve, you can then trace the main water supply and see where it goes. Notice that one pipe enters the top of the heater, that is, if your house is heated by radiators. Another pipe will go into the water heater. Other pipes will go up into the house at various places.

From the water heater a second pipe also goes into the house. If you feel this pipe, it is warm to the touch, for it carries the hot water, after it has been heated, to wherever it is needed.

Along one wall of your house, probably fairly close to the floor, you will see a very large pipe. This is the waste pipe, which varies in size from four to eight inches in diameter. If you trace the waste pipe back, you will find that at one point it is joined by another pipe of about the same size that is coming down from the upper floors. This is the stack, which carries the wastes from the various fixtures to the waste pipe.

It's easy to see how plumbing makes life more convenient and pleasant. At home we use water for drinking, cooking, heating the rooms, operating the toilet, washing the clothes, and cleaning the house and the people in it. Just think how your life would be changed if you had to go outdoors to bring in the water for all these tasks.

THE HEATING SYSTEM

The second great convenience of the American home is the central heating plant which permits us to have controlled temperatures at all times. In many parts of the world, people are able to live in cold climates because they heat their homes with fire.

Fire as a source of heat is certainly not a new invention. Very early man didn't need heat because he lived in warm climates. But after he discovered how to make fires, he was able to move into cooler climates throughout the world.

The water heater

Later, cave man used fire to keep himself warm, to light his cave, and to protect himself from savage beasts. Primitive man burned fire in an open hearth in the center of his dwelling. Men who live in a primitive way in today's world do the same thing.

The ancient Romans were the first to develop the idea of central heating. In the *atrium,* the central room of a Roman house, a fire was built, and the heat from it was carried by pipes to other rooms.

THE FIREPLACE

The idea of central heating was not taken up by the people of succeeding cultures, most of whom built fires at the center of the house and permitted the smoke to escape through a hole in the roof. Gradually, the hearth was moved from the center of the room to one side. Later, the fires were enclosed, making fireplaces, which were used to heat most houses in the western world until the nineteenth century. Only then did people begin to use stoves, such as the Franklin stove, which was invented by Benjamin Franklin.

A Franklin stove

In some places before the coming of central heating, sleeping rooms were not heated, and cold beds were warmed before bedtime by placing in them hot bricks from the fireplace. Hot bricks were also used to warm the feet of those who traveled by carriage or sleigh on cold winter days.

The main disadvantage of heating with a fireplace or stove is that each room must have its own heating unit. In other words, if you had a ten room house, you would need ten fireplaces to heat all of it. As a result, many homeowners heated only some of the rooms and left the others cold. Usually, the heated rooms were those used during the day. The bedrooms were not heated because sleepers could use blankets to keep themselves warm at night.

Today many houses still get their warmth from fireplaces. In others a stove of some kind is used, while still others use a gas ring, a heating unit that consists of a ring with holes through which gas flows and is burned. Some houses are also warmed by electric units that heat a single room. But in many parts of the world people still heat their dwellings with open fires.

THE STEAM SYSTEM

Our present-day central heating systems usually use either steam, hot water, or hot air.

In a steam system, heat changes the water in the boiler to steam. This then pushes its way through pipes into radiators which are placed throughout the house. The radiators are equipped with valves at one end to permit the air to escape as steam fills the radiator. Once inside the radiator, the steam begins to lose its heat and condenses into water. Then, by means of return pipes, it goes back to the heater.

Heating by steam is very efficient. Its advantage is that since only a small amount of water need be used, it can be quickly heated to a very high temperature. Thus it can bring a cold house to a comfortable temperature in a short space of time. One of the disadvantages of steam heat is that the radiators get to be quite hot when steam is in them, and anyone touching a hot radiator can feel real pain, but today most such radiators are covered. Another disadvantage is that steam heat tends to be noisy. The pipes clunk and clank, and the valves constantly hiss, but even these can be comfortable sounds on a very cold day.

A radiator

THE HOT WATER SYSTEM

Hot water heat is similar to steam in that fire heats the water in a boiler, but much more water must be used than is needed for steam heat. After the water is boiled, it circulates through the radiators as hot water, warming them and thereby the house. As in a steam system, when the water circulates, it loses its heat, becomes cooler, and returns to the boiler to be heated again.

During the summer months, when the hot water heater is not operating, the water in the system contracts as it cools and takes up less space. This permits an air pocket to form in the radiators Before the heater can be operated efficiently again for the colder months, this air must be removed. Simple needle valves are placed at one end of the radiator to permit this. As the water fills up the radiator, it forces the air out of the valve.

THE HOT AIR SYSTEM

In a hot air system, the heater warms air that is carried by large pipes called *ducts* to various parts of the house where it enters rooms through openings known as *registers*. Occasionally, the air is forced through the system by blowers which are simply fans placed at the heat source.

Different fuels are used in the various heating systems. Coal was once the most commonly used,

but it was very dirty and polluted the air. Now oil and gas are the more commonly used fuels.

Electric heaters are efficient, but are not widely used because they are expensive. Although experiments are going on in the use of solar heaters (units operated by the heat of the sun), several problems must still be solved. On cloudy days and at night, some other heat source must be used. The units, too, are very expensive, but work is being done to reduce this cost. Successful solar ovens have been used for cooking and for scientific experiments.

But let's go down into the basement and look at your heater. If it is one that heats either steam or hot water, the water pipe that you followed coming into the house has a branch that goes into the top of the heater. If you feel this pipe, it will

The coal being shoveled into this furnace provides good heat — and a great deal of dirt.

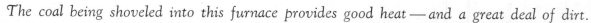

50

be cold, for it brings into the system the water to be heated.

Another pipe can be seen coming out of the heater and going up into the house. This, if it is part of a hot water system, will be warm all the time. If it is a steam system, it is sometimes cold and sometimes very, very hot. So don't touch it!

THE FURNACE

If your furnace uses oil or gas, the fuel will enter it through a pipe near the bottom of the heater. If it is a coal furnace, the coal probably has to be shoveled in.

A coal furnace has two doors at the front. Open the upper door and you will see the bed of flame. It is through this door that the coal must be shoveled in order to feed the fire. Below is another door. Here the draft is permitted to enter and to circulate beneath the fire to keep it burning. This is also the place from which the burnt ashes are removed.

Toward the top of the heater you will see a gauge. In a hot water system, the gauge shows how much water is in the boiler and pipes. In a steam system, the gauge shows what the steam pressure is.

HOT AIR AND WATER FURNACES

In a hot air system the bed of flame again is at the bottom of the furnace. The pipes coming out of the top carry the heated air to the ducts which circulate it throughout the house. The hot air pipes are very large in comparison with those at the top of the steam and hot water systems; such pipes are often more than a foot in diameter. This system is very popular in many modern houses, especially those in which air conditioning is planned, for the ducts can also be used to circulate cool air for air conditioning units during the summer months.

Although the hot air or water in these systems is often helped along its way by blowers or circulators, this is not always the case. Because the air or water is heated matter, it tends to circulate naturally, without any additional help. How does this come about?

When any matter is heated, the tiny molecules which make it up move about faster and faster as they take on more heat. At the same time, they move farther away from each other. This means that a cubic foot of heated matter would have fewer molecules in it than a cubic foot of cooler matter. As a result, the heated matter would weigh less than a cubic foot of cooler matter.

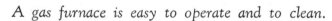

A gas furnace is easy to operate and to clean.

Some Experiments

Check with your parents before you do the experiments in the following pages. Always have a grownup present while an experiment is being carried out.

Let us see how this happens. Take some safety matches, and on a sheet of paper draw two squares.

 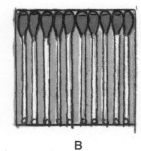

Make each side of the squares as long as one match. Now take the matches and place them in the squares so that each holds the same number of matches.

Let's pretend that each of the matchsticks represents one molecule. Let's pretend further that

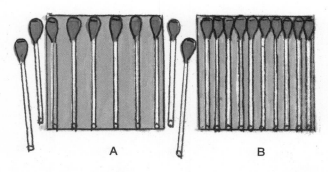

we have heated those in square A. Heated molecules move away from each other, so we should now separate the matches in square A by about one-eight of an inch. Because there is no room for expansion within the square, some molecules must move outside the square.

The two squares take up the same amount of space, but square A now has fewer molecules (matches) than square B. If the squares were weighed, square B, having more molecules, would be heavier than A. If the squares represented units of air or water, square B, being heavier, would sink, and square A, being lighter, would rise to the top.

This is what happens when air or water is warmed in a heating system. The heated air, being lighter, rises and circulates through the system. As it moves through the house it loses heat, becomes cooler and thus heavier, returns to the heater, and is reheated.

The same thing happens to the air in a room as you will see in this experiment. Take a piece of punk and light an end of it. After it is burning well, blow out the flame. The punk will continue to smoke. Now take it, still smoking, and hold it at the bottom of a hot radiator. Notice that the smoke blows toward the radiator and then goes up.

Next hold the punk above the radiator. As you will see, the smoke now goes straight up.

The arrows show how

If you open the refrigerator and hold the punk at the bottom, you will see that the smoke moves downward because the air in the refrigerator is cooler and thus heavier than the air in the room.

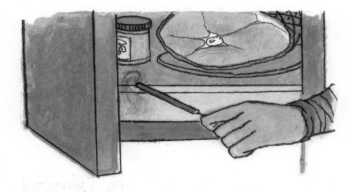

Now remove an ice tray and hold the punk under it. As the hot smoke rises it hits the bottom of the tray where, being cooled by the cold tray, it begins to move downward.

This series of little experiments shows how air circulates in a room. The cool air, being heavier,

the air circulates in a room.

is at the bottom of the room. When it touches any heating unit, such as a radiator, it is heated and rises toward the ceiling. Here it cools off, gets heavier, and returns to the floor, where it again comes in contact with the heating unit. Rising toward the ceiling, it once again circulates around the room. Such circulation of air continues constantly.

With the smoking punk you saw how air expands and rises when heated. Here is an experiment to show how the same thing happens with heated water. Find a large jar and a small bottle. The jar must be large enough for the bottle to sit comfortably inside of it.

Make a snug-fitting stopper for the small bottle out of a cork. Through the stopper, bore a hole large enough to hold a plastic straw.

Now fill the small bottle with water, adding a little color to make the water easier to see.

Force the straw through the cork stopper, and then squeeze the stopper and straw onto the top of the bottle. Some of the liquid should move up into the straw. With a magic marker, make a line on the straw where the colored water stops.

Place the small bottle in the larger jar. Boil some water and pour it into the jar so that it completely surrounds the bottle. What happens to the colored water in the straw? Notice that as

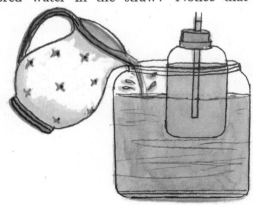

the colored water takes on heat, it rises above the mark you've made on the straw. Again you have demonstrated that when heated, matter expands.

HEAT-CONDUCTION

Why are radiators made of metal? Why not fashion them out of wood so that they may better match the furniture? Metal is used because it is a good conductor of heat.

Have you ever gone into the bathroom and sat in the tub before drawing the water? If so, you probably noticed how very cold the tub felt. It seemed much colder than other things in the room. Had you sat on a wooden floor, for instance, it wouldn't have seemed nearly so cold. And yet, the temperature of each was the same. Both were at room temperature.

Why did the tub seem so much colder than the floor? The answer is that the tub, being made of iron, a very good conductor of heat, removed the heat from your body at a much faster rate than did the floor, a poor conductor of heat. Thus the tub seemed cold and the floor much warmer.

Whenever your mother bakes cookies, she is always very careful when removing them from the oven to use a pot holder. If she were to touch the cookie sheet with her bare hand a severe burn might result. At the same time she is able to pick up one of the cookies and taste it. The cookies and the cookie sheet are naturally the same temperature. However, because the cookie sheet is made of

metal, a good heat conductor, it transfers the heat to the hand more rapidly than does the cookie, a poor conductor, and therefore can cause a bad burn.

AN EXPERIMENT

Let's try an experiment to show the difference in the heat conductivity of metal and wood. At the hardware store, buy a short length of iron rod and a wooden dowel of the same length and thickness. After you've brought them home, light a candle and burn it until the wax begins to melt. Let one drop of wax fall at an end of the dowel and another drop at an end of the metal rod.

Insert the other ends of the rod and dowel

into a pot of boiling water. Notice how quickly the wax on the metal rod melts. The wax on the dowel will not melt for a long time. This shows that metal can conduct heat more rapidly than can wood. It is for this reason that many cooking pots have handles made of wood, while the main part of the pot is made of metal.

ELECTRICITY

The third reason that the modern home is superior in convenience and comfort to the homes of long ago is the use of electricity. The existence of electricity was known long ago when the ancient Greeks discovered that if fur were rubbed against amber, the amber could pick up little straws. Magnetism of this sort is called *static electricity*.

Michael Faraday

oped a cell that could produce electricity. Before that, there had been no way of storing electricity and no electrical source that could keep a light burning for any length of time. But Volta's battery was too expensive for general use.

In 1831, Michael Farraday, an English scientist, developed his theory of magnetic induction. He

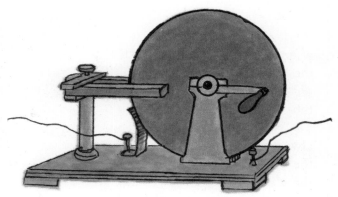

Michael Faraday's Generator

As long ago as 1650, Otto Von Guericke produced a form of electric light by holding his hand against a rapidly rotating sulphur globe, causing it to glow. In the beginning of the eighteenth century, Francis Hauksbee produced the first electric light, and in 1802, Sir Humphrey Davy produced the arc lamp, but this gave such a strong light that it could not be used in the home. However, these experiments were merely interesting discoveries in the history of lighting when compared with the work of the Italian Allesandro Volta, who devel-

was able to get electricity to flow through a wire by passing it through a magnetic field. This principle permitted the development of the generator, the machine we use today to make most of our electricity.

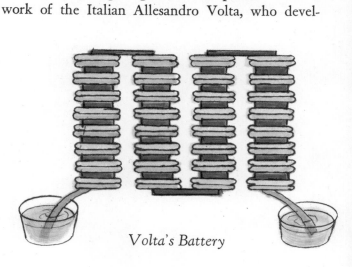

Volta's Battery

Alessandro Volta

Thomas Edison and the Electric Bulb

During the latter part of the nineteenth century, many people produced versions of electric lights, but it was not until 1879 that the American Thomas Edison invented the first really practical electric light. It was called the *incandescent lamp*, from a Latin word meaning *to glow*. Edison had spent $40,000 as well as a great deal of time in the development of his light—and $40,000 was a considerable sum of money in 1879.

The bulb, which looks so simple, makes us wonder why so much time and money were needed to perfect it. Edison's idea was that if he passed electricity through certain substances they would get hot enough to glow. To do this, he reduced various substances to the thickness of a fine thread, or *filament*. Edison was able to get the filaments to glow, but they got so hot that they just burned up.

Since burning requires oxygen, Edison enclosed a filament in a globe and pumped all the air

In addition to the electric bulb, Thomas Alva Edison invented the phonograph, the microphone, and hundreds of other objects that he thought were "needed or wanted."

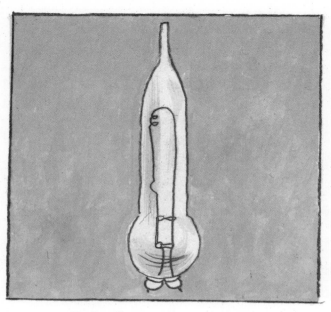

Early German lamp (1854)

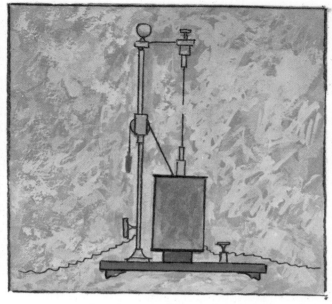

An arc-type lamp (1848)

from it. This experiment was successful, and the filament glowed without burning.

Next, Edison had to find which material was best for his filament. After experimenting with various woods, he finally came up with a carbon filament made with bamboo fibers. It glowed with a soft white light inside his vacuum globe. This was the first incandescent lamp.

After the invention of the electric light, practical uses of electricity began to develop rapidly. Inventions of all sorts came onto the market, and Edison himself was credited with over a thousand. Some of his best known are the phonograph, the motion picture, and the microphone.

Edison lamp (1879)

HOUSEKEEPING WITH ELECTRICITY

When your grandmother was a young woman, she probably used a broom and carpet beater to clean her floors and rugs. Now all this work is done with a vacuum cleaner, made possible because the modern house is an electrical house.

At one time, heavy carpets had to be carried outdoors, hung on a line, and then beaten to give them a good cleaning. Today the job is done just as well and more easily by the vacuum cleaner.

All of the above are powered by electricity.

Above: A fireplace

Below: A coal stove

An electric range

The people of colonial times did their cooking over kitchen fireplaces. Later, coal-burning stoves were the ranges that were used for cooking. But now your mother can do all of her cooking on an electric range. She can even put her food in the oven and go off to do her shopping, after having set the electric range to go on at a certain time and do her cooking while she is out.

Think of how different our houses would be without electricity. We use electricity for ceiling lights, lamps, room heaters, radios, television sets, electric fans, vacuum cleaners, air conditioners, ranges, refrigerators, mixers, toasters, coffee makers, waffle irons, roasters, hot water heaters, washing machines, irons, and many, many other things.

Outside the home, electricity is used to operate lighthouses, traffic lights, trains, and many other

things too numerous to list here. Without electricity, modern industry would come to a standstill.

The Fuse Box

To learn something about the electricity in your own house, take one more trip to the basement or utility room. There you can trace the wires bearing the electricity into the house.

Probably toward the front of the building you will see a very heavy wire or cable coming through the wall. In all probability, it is shielded in metal. Inside the house, this cable goes to a meter that measures the amount of electricity used.

After leaving the meter, the main line goes to the main fuse box where it passes through the main fuse or circuit breaker. Inside the fuse box, the current is divided among many different lines which go to various parts of the house. Each of

these lines has a certain number of electrical fixtures planned for it, and each line also has its own fuse. Thus, should one line become overloaded only the fuse for that line will blow, allowing the rest of the lines to function normally. Some lines may have ten or fifteen fixtures operating from them. Others may have only one, depending upon how much current the appliance pulls. An electric range, for instance, having a very strong heating unit, would have its own line with its own fuse, but a reading lamp would be on a line with a great many other appliances because the lamp uses a small current.

From the main fuse box on all sides, you will see a great many wires, all much smaller than the main line, coming from and going to various parts of the house. These are the individual circuits. Although one line may go to several rooms, each room should be serviced by at least two lines. This makes it possible to have light in each room even when one of the fuses has blown.

Opening a fuse box can be very dangerous.

The main line enters the fuse box.

Experiments with the Complete Electric Circuit

How does electricity make an appliance work? In order for electricity to flow, there must be what is called "a complete circuit." This involves having the current running from the source of electricity through the appliance and back to the ground. If the current is not permitted to do this by breaking the line somewhere along the route, no current will flow. This fact is used in the construction of switches.

Here's an experiment. Take a dry cell battery, two pieces of electrical wire each about a foot long, two pieces of wood three and six inches square respectively, three wood screws, a flashlight bulb, and

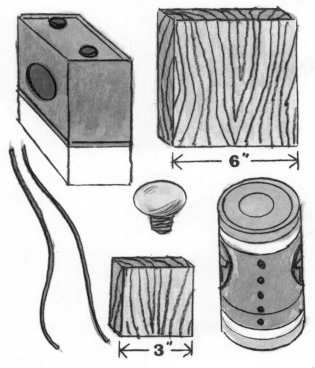

a tin can. *Put on work gloves; this is important.* With a pair of metal shears, cut from the can a piece of metal one inch wide and four inches long. Cut a second strip one inch wide by two inches long.

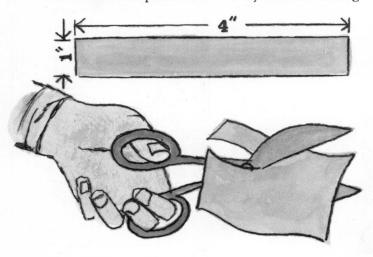

Drill a hole through each end of the smaller strip of metal. These holes should be just large enough for the wood screws. Drill a similar hole at one end of the larger metal strip. At the other end of this strip, drill a hole into which a flashlight bulb can be screwed.

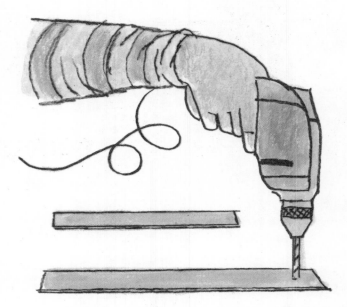

Nail the smaller block of wood into the larger one, as shown. Passing the wood screws through the

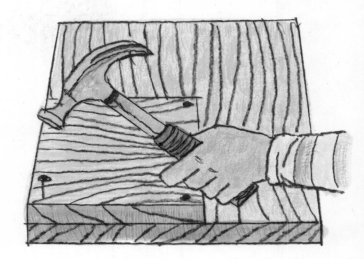

holes, attach the smaller piece of metal to the large block of wood, as in the picture. With the remaining

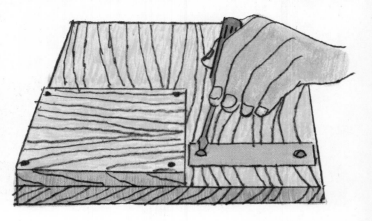

screw, attach the larger metal strip to the smaller piece of wood so that the large hole is directly over the first piece of metal.

Screw the bulb through the large hole, making sure that the bottom of it touches the metal strip beneath. Attach one end of one wire to terminal A

of the battery. Loosen screw C somewhat and wrap the other end of the wire around it. Tighten the screw. What happens? Does the light go on? No?

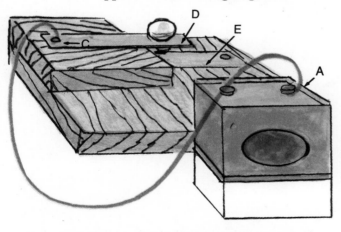

The reason the bulb remains off is that, although electricity seems to be coming from the battery to screw C, along metal strip D, and into the bulb,

nothing is really happening at all. A complete circuit has not been made. In order to complete the circuit, the current must be returned to the other terminal, the ground terminal of the battery.

To complete the circuit, take the second wire and wrap one end around terminal B of the battery. Attach the other end of the wire to screw F. Does the light go on now? Of course! You have completed

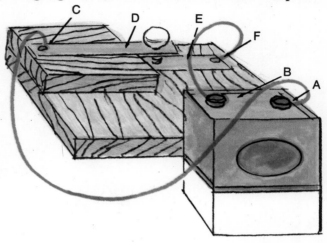

the circuit. The electricity passes from terminal A through the wire to screw C, into the strip of metal D, and into the light bulb. It then passes through the light bulb and travels along the metal strip E to screw F. From F it goes along the wire and back to the battery at terminal B, completing the circuit.

If you move the light bulb with your finger away from metal strip E, what happens? The light goes out because you have broken the circuit and no electricity is flowing anywhere. Permit the bulb to

snap back so that it touches the metal again. The light goes on because once again you have a completed circuit. If you permit it to remain this way, the light will stay on until it burns out or the battery loses its power.

This is not what happens in your house, because there the lights are not always turned on; you have switches to turn them off. Everytime you turn off a switch, you break the circuit.

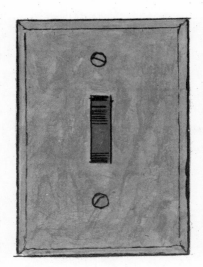

hole in it at one end and attach it to the block of

How to Make a Light Switch

As we have seen in the previous experiment, no electrical appliance will work unless a complete circuit exists. Should the circuit be broken at any point the appliance will stop functioning. This fact is used in the construction of on and off switches.

Perhaps we should construct a light switch. You will need another three-inch square of wood, a third

wood with a screw. Underneath the raised metal, put a screw into the wood block.

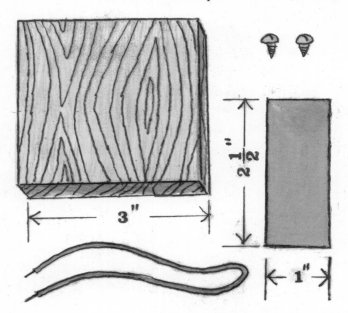

piece of wire a foot long, and another strip of metal one inch wide by about 2½ inches long. Bend the piece of metal, as shown below. Then drill a

Take the battery used on page 62; remove the wire going to terminal B and attach it to screw G. Connect one end of the third piece of wire I

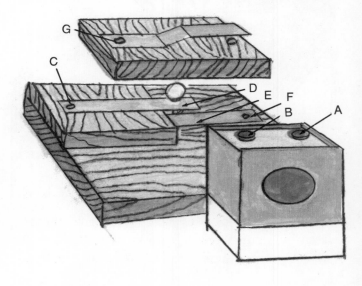

and the other end to the battery terminal B. Now is the light on? No? Why is that?

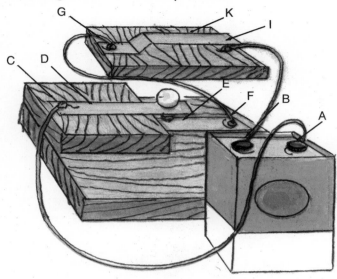

Let's trace what is happening. The current can go from terminal A to C, through D, into the light bulb, through E to F and on to G. But once it arrives in the metal strip K, it has nowhere to go. The circuit, therefore, is not complete.

Now, with your finger, depress metal piece K so that it touches screw I beneath it. Does the light

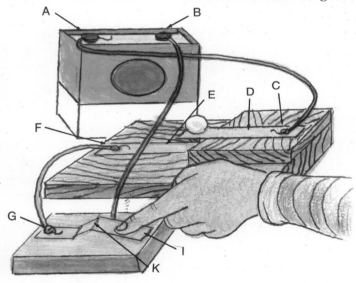

go on? Certainly! You have a complete circuit, for when the current went into K it could move on to screw I and along the wire back to the battery at terminal B. This is what happens with your house light switch.

The Electromagnet

Over a hundred years ago, scientists discovered that if you passed electricity through a wire, you created a magnetic field around that wire. By wrap-

ping wire around a core of some kind, they found that it was possible to create a powerful magnet which could be turned off and on at will. This device was called an *electromagnet*.

In order to demonstrate, let's create our own electromagnet. Wind the middle part of a two foot long piece of wire around a flat-headed, two-inch

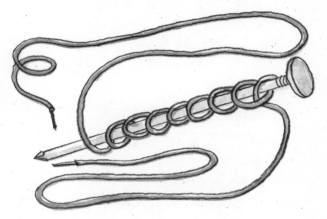

nail, as shown in the picture. Connect the two ends of the wire to the two terminals of the battery. Now,

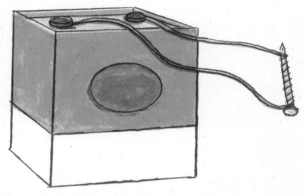

take the wrapped nail and bring it near a thumb tack. Does anything happen? The nail acts like a magnet and attracts the tack to it. Remove one of

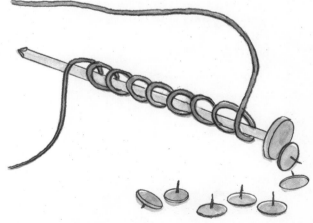

the wires from the battery terminal. You have broken the circuit. Is the nail any longer magnetic? Naturally not, because no current is present in the wire. Connect the wire back to the battery, and the nail once again becomes a magnet.

A doorbell

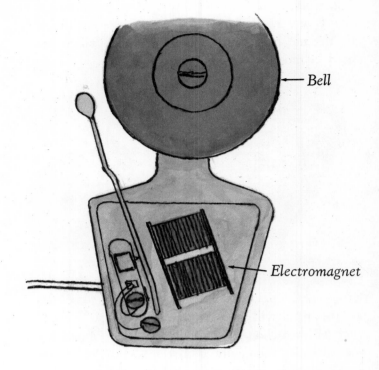

Bell

Electromagnet

HOW A DOORBELL WORKS

Electromagnets are used for many things. One that you probably use every day is in your door bell. When you push the button, the electricity flows through the coils of an electromagnet which is mounted in the bell opposite the clapper, the piece of metal which actually strikes the bell.

When the electromagnet becomes magnetized it draws the clapper over against itself and away from a contact point. When this happens the cir-

Clapper

Contact point

Electromagnet

cuit is broken because the clapper must touch the contact point in order to keep the current flowing.

As soon as the circuit is broken, the clapper snaps back into its position against the contact point. Of course this makes the circuit complete once again and the current begins to flow through the coils of the electromagnet, setting up a magnetic field. The clapper is drawn to the electromagnet a second time, and so the cycle begins again.

This alteration from a complete to an incomplete circuit continues for as long as the finger remains on the button. Each time that the clapper springs back from the electromagnet, one end, containing a small hammerhead, strikes the bell, making it ring.

THE FUSE

Fires are often caused by faulty wiring in houses. The wiring in some old houses had rubber as its insulation. Through the years the rubber had dried out and flaked off, exposing the bare wire. If two bare wires going to and from a fixture should touch each other, a short circuit results.

A short circuit in a system with a dry cell battery is not particularly dangerous because the amount of current is small. However, in a regular house circuit it can be dangerous since the amount of current is much greater and the wires can get very hot. If they should touch something flammable, such as a rug, while in this hot condition, they could start a fire. One way we have of helping to prevent this is by the use of circuit breakers or fuses, which are used in most houses today.

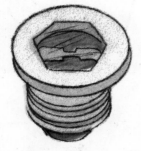

A fuse

The current passes through the fuse, which is a small strip of soft metal with a low melting point. Should the system become overloaded so that the wires heat up, the piece of metal in the fuse also heats, and it will melt long before the regular wires can get hot enough to do any damage. When the metal melts, the circuit is broken and the electricity ceases to flow, eliminating the danger.

Here the central part melted, breaking the circuit.

Let's Make a Fuse

Shall we make a fuse to see how it works? You will need a three-inch square of wood and the foil wrapper from a stick of gum. Cut the foil into the

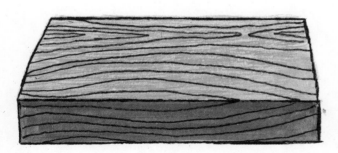

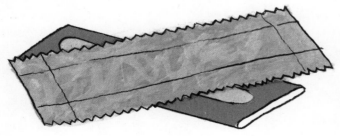

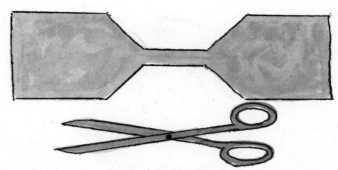

shape shown in the picture. Place it on the block of wood and screw it down with wood screws at

each end. Run a wire from one screw to a terminal of the battery, and a second wire from the other screw to the second terminal of the battery. The foil

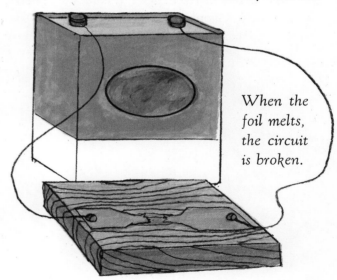

When the foil melts, the circuit is broken.

gets warm. Eventually it melts. This is exactly what happens with a house fuse.

If you had a light anywhere on the circuit it would go out. The reason that the fuse has blown is that there is a short circuit. The current passed from terminal A of the battery to terminal B without going through any fixtures.

The Modern Castle

We have looked in some detail at our modern home. It is superior to those of other times, not because it is bigger and grander, not because it has rooms with fancy plasterwork on the walls, and not because it has armies of servants obeying its owner as if he were a king of an ancient kingdom. But the citizen of today does indeed have servants of a special kind. They are not people, but the inventions of people, and they are run by electricity.

The dweller in today's modern home can, by flicking a switch, have his home heated or cooled, his rooms lighted, his floors cleaned, and his clothes washed. He can be entertained by his stereophonograph, his radio, or his television set. Although the average citizen of the western world is not a king or queen, he lives in his own castle in more comfort than any king of other days, and his castle is the modern home.

Some Other Books to Read